D0432224

APR 1 4

The Planets

Your Mission to Mercury

by Christine Zuchora-Walske
illustrated by Scott Burroughs

Content Consultant
Diane M. Bollen, Research Scientist,
Cornell University

magic wagon

visit us at www.abdopublishing.com

Printed in the United States of America, North Mankato, Minnesota.
052011
092011
 THIS BOOK CONTAINS AT LEAST 10% RECYCLED MATERIALS.

Text by Christine Zuchora-Walske
Illustrations by Scott Burroughs
Edited by Holly Saari
Series design and cover production by Becky Daum
Interior production by Christa Schneider

Library of Congress Cataloging-in-Publication Data
Zuchora-Walske, Christine.
  Your mission to Mercury / by Christine Zuchora-Walske ; illustrated by Scott Burroughs.
     p. cm. — (The planets)
  Includes index.
  ISBN 978-1-61641-680-5
  1. Mercury (Planet)—Juvenile literature. 2. Mercury (Planet)—Exploration—Juvenile literature. 3. Solar system—Juvenile literature. I. Burroughs, Scott, ill. II. Title.
  QB611.Z83 2012
  523.41—dc22
                          2011006776

Table of Contents

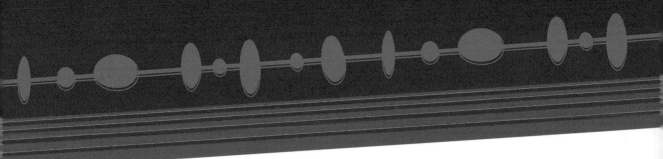

Imagine You Could Go

You couldn't really visit Mercury. It does not have enough oxygen for you to breathe. The daytime heat would burn you to a crisp. The night's cold would freeze you to death.

Nobody has ever traveled to Mercury. But imagine if you could . . .

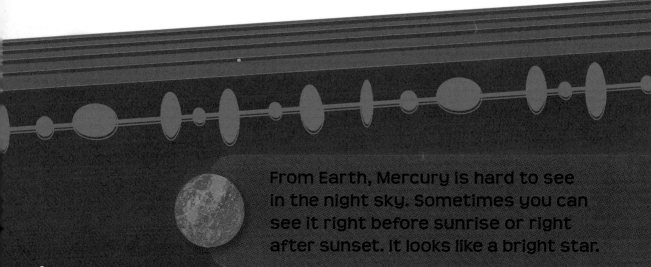

From Earth, Mercury is hard to see in the night sky. Sometimes you can see it right before sunrise or right after sunset. It looks like a bright star.

MERCURY
VENUS
EARTH
MARS
JUPITER
SATURN
URANUS
NEPTUNE

SUN

THE
SOLAR SYSTEM

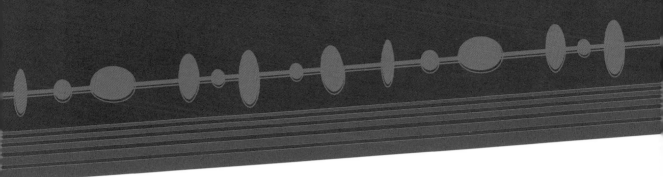

Solar System

To find your way, you carry a map of our solar system. Your map shows eight planets orbiting the sun. Mercury is the planet closest to the sun.

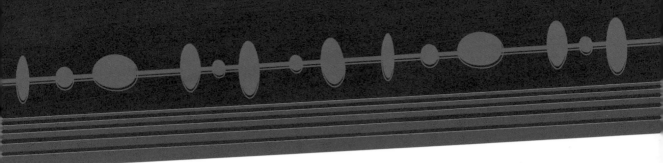

Small Planet

Mercury is the smallest planet in our solar system. About 18 of the planets squished together would make one Earth.

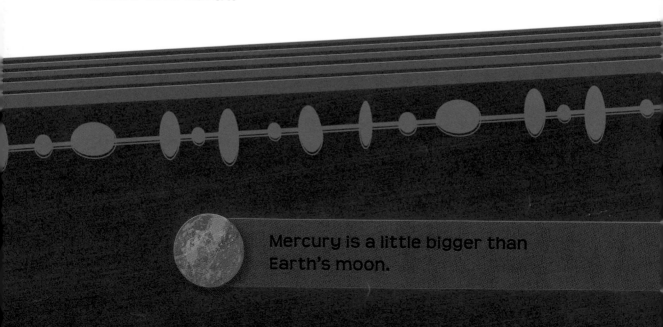

Mercury is a little bigger than Earth's moon.

SIZE COMPARISON

EARTH'S MOON

MERCURY

EARTH

9

Distance from Earth

The average distance between Earth and Mercury is about 57 million miles (92 million km). Luckily, you get to travel in the world's fastest rocket. But it will still take a few months to get there. You get out your books and puzzles for the long trip.

Years and Days

During your trip, you brush up on your Mercury facts. You remember that a year is the time it takes for a planet to orbit the sun once. One Earth year is 365 days. What is Mercury's year? It's much shorter at only 88 days!

Mercury got its name because of its speedy orbit. Ancient people named this planet after their god Mercury, who wore winged shoes and a winged hat.

TODAY'S
TO DO
LIST...

14

Planets don't just orbit the sun. They also spin like tops. That spinning is what causes the sun to appear and disappear in the sky each day.

The time it takes between each sunrise on Earth is 24 hours. On Mercury, you'll have to wait about 176 Earth days for the next sunrise. What will you do during the long Mercury days?

Mercury's Appearance

Your spacecraft finally draws close to Mercury. You gaze out the window. Mercury looks like Earth's moon. The ground is rocky. You see a long, jagged crack. That must be a cliff where the ground drops down.

You see craters everywhere. Some are small and some are large. The larger ones slope down like shallow bowls. You steer your spacecraft toward a flat, sunny plain. You carefully land your craft.

Less Gravity, No Atmosphere

You climb out of your spacecraft. Your body feels light. That's because Mercury's gravity is weaker than Earth's.

You look up and see the blackness of space. Earth's atmosphere scatters the sun's light, making the beautiful blue sky. But Mercury has almost no atmosphere. So the light doesn't scatter. Mercury's sky is always black. You also see the sun. It looks three times as big as it looks from Earth.

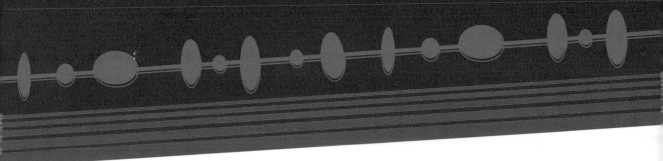

Surface

You hop in your rover. You head toward the Caloris Basin. This basin is Mercury's biggest landform. It's about the size of Texas. The basin formed when a meteorite crashed into Mercury almost 4 billion years ago. Mountains surround the Caloris Basin.

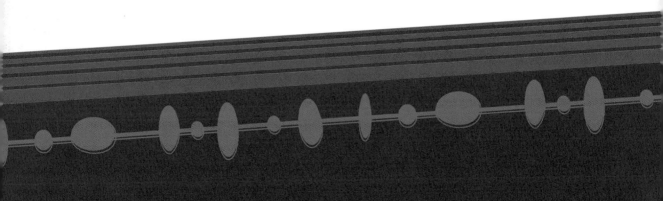

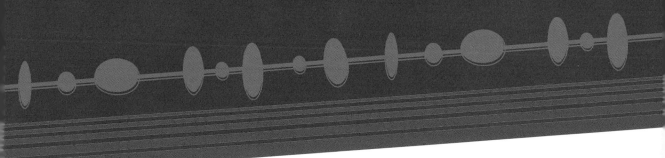

Next, you head for Discovery Rupes. This is a long, high cliff. It's about one mile (1.6 km) high. The cliff is twice as tall as Earth's tallest building.

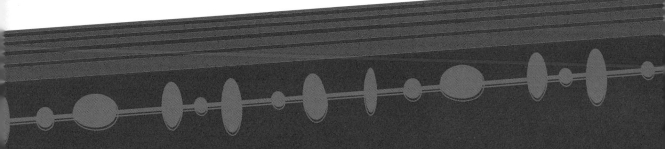

Mercury's cliffs formed because the planet shrank. As Mercury shrank, its surface wrinkled. The wrinkles are the cliffs.

Temperature

Now you drive to the dark side of Mercury. That's the side that faces away from the sun. Because the planet spins so slowly, one side stays dark for a long time. It's freezing cold here. Mercury has almost no atmosphere to hold in heat. Temperatures can drop to –279 degrees Fahrenheit (–173°C).

Next, you go to Mercury's north pole. Scientists have asked you to find some answers for them. They know ice exists at both of Mercury's poles. Where did it come from? Can you find a clue?

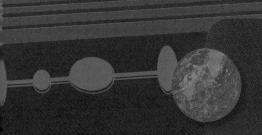

Nobody knows how Mercury got its ice. Steam may have seeped up from Mercury's hot core. As it cooled, the steam could have turned into liquid and froze into ice.

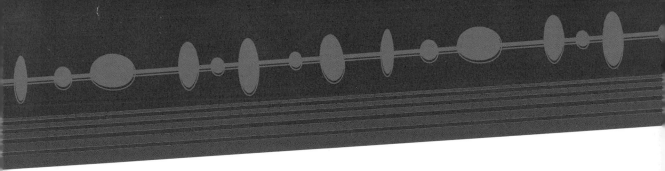

Core

You've saved your toughest job for last. You want to see what Mercury's core is made of. You drill down beneath Mercury's rocky surface. You find iron. But the iron is so hot that it is liquid. Mercury's core is huge. It makes up about three-fourths of the planet's diameter.

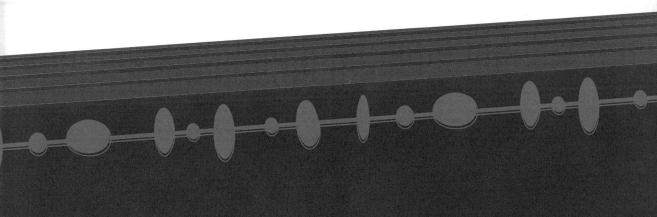

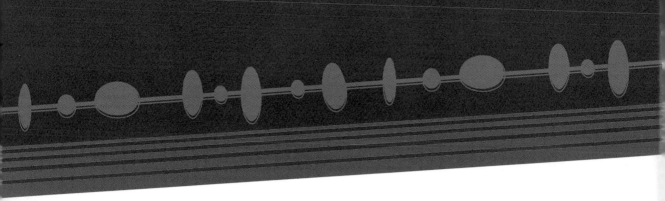

An Amazing Trip

You climb back up to Mercury's surface. You're tired and dirty. But you don't care. You've seen amazing sights on Mercury!

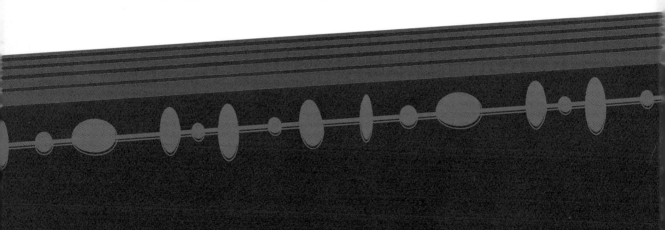

How Do Scientists Know about Mercury?

Astronomers have been watching Mercury for thousands of years. Early people studied Mercury with the naked eye. In 1631, French scientist Pierre Gassendi studied the planet with a telescope. For the next three centuries, scientists continued to study Mercury through telescopes.

In the 1960s, scientists began using radar to observe the planet. Radar is electronic signals that travel through the air. In 1965, scientists found out how fast Mercury spins. Until then, everyone thought that Mercury always kept the same face toward the sun, just as Earth's moon does toward Earth.

In 1974, *Mariner 10* became the first spacecraft to reach Mercury. It carried no astronauts. It took the first close-up pictures of Mercury's surface. It also measured temperatures on the surface and discovered that Mercury has a large iron core.

In 2004, scientists sent a second spacecraft, *Messenger*, to Mercury. *Messenger* flew by Mercury three times and took pictures of almost all of its surface. The next mission to Mercury is called *BepiColombo*. It is scheduled to launch in 2013.

Mercury Facts

Position: First planet from sun

Distance from sun: 36 million miles (58 million km)

Diameter (distance through the planet's middle): 3,032 miles (4,879 km)

Length of orbit (year): 88 Earth days

Length of day (from sunrise to sunrise): About 176 Earth days

Gravity: Less than half as strong as Earth's gravity

Number of moons: 0

Words to Know

atmosphere—the layer of gases surrounding a planet.

basin—a large dip in a planet's surface.

core—the center of a planet.

crater—a dip in the ground shaped like a large bowl.

gravity—the force that pulls a smaller object toward a larger object.

meteorite—a chunk of rock from space that has crashed into a planet.

orbit—to travel around something, usually in an oval path.

solar system—a star and the objects, such as planets, that travel around it.

Learn More

Books

Jefferis, David. *Hot Planets*. New York: Crabtree, 2008.

Landau, Elaine. *Mercury*. New York: Children's Press, 2008.

Yasuda, Anita. *Explore the Solar System!* White River Junction, VT: Nomad Press, 2009.

Web Sites

To learn more about Mercury, visit ABDO Group online at **www.abdopublishing.com**. Web sites about Mercury are featured on our Book Links page. These links are routinely monitored and updated to provide the most current information available.

Index